THE RIVER'S DAUGHTER
POEMS

TERRY HERMSEN

BOTTOM DOG PRESS
HURON, OHIO

© 2008
Terry Hermsen
Bottom Dog Press
PO Box 425 / Huron, OH 44839
http://members.aol.com/Lsmithdog/bottomdog

ISBN 978-1-933964-20-1
ISBN 1-933964-20-0

Cover & Author Photos by Nelson Strong, "Zion Reflections"©
Cover & Interior Layout by Susanna Sharp-Schwacke

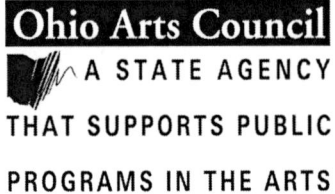

Bottom Dog Press

Huron, Ohio

Contents

The Touch of Strangers
For Samuel, at Seven Months 10
Starved Rock 12
Children's Drawings 14
The Baboushka Poems 15
The River's Daughter 19
The Theft of Silk 23
Notes from a Season along the Olentangy 24
The Good House 26

Summer by Summer
Half-Sonnet: Sunday 28
Sea Turtle 29
Train and Ocean 30
Singing to Noah 31
Watching Isa Pitch 32
Train to Glacier 33
This Day's Thirst 35
Solstice at Kendall Ridges 36
Skipping Stones with Noah 38
Bagworms in Their Tent Above the River 39

Eight Riddles
For the Day 42
Limbic Construction 43
The Deceivers 44
Incantation for Departure 45
Two-Headed Cadence 46
Courting the Address 47
The Accordion 48
Lessons in Trust 49
Clues & Answers 50

Cross-State
Driving Northeast on Route 42, I Cross Under a Double Rainbow 52
In the Fields of Oil 53
My Mother Above the Abandoned Quarry 56
One More Rainy Morning 57
Construction 59
The Yellow Spring 60
Cross-State 62
After August 63
The Paris Room 64

Eight Inkblots

In This Tavern 69
Mr. Double-Eyes 71
Combatants 73
The Rivering 75
Scarab 77
The Forest Floor 79
Trumpeters 81
Dance of the Single-Winged 83

Disappearances

The Mayor's Promise 86
The Satyr and the Peasants 87
Child Aloft in Ohio Theater 88
Terra Haute 89
Another Fourth 90
Four Psalms 91
Ghazal 93
Credo 94
To Eakins 96
Driving Home 97

Mimesis

Mimesis: The Nighthawk 100
Prairie Burn 101
Path to the River 103
Wheatfield, July 105
One Love 107
Because of Your White Shoulder 109
At Isa Lake: An Epithalamium 110
Pegasus 111
Love Poem, August 112

Acknowledgements 115
About the Author 117

For Isa
and all those I have loved...

*"One day they will meet, they will assemble
like guests with the visors up,*

*and here on earth, not in heaven,
as in a house filled with music ..."*
-Osip Mandelstam

1.
THE TOUCH OF STRANGERS

*"Green water of lagoons,
brown water of a great river ...*

          *the great body
not torn apart, though raked and raked
by our claws—"*
        -Denise Levertov

For Samuel, at Seven Months

The moon from its western perch
on some magician strings
dips behind several jagged
dragons-tail clouds.

This is the flatland, Samuel,
pre-dawn chilly April.
Like every morning, I ride my bike
through the monstrous sprawl of town.

A rain begins: I hitch my collar higher.
A close car starts, the stars are going.
Months ago you turned in your mother's belly.
Does the flowing earth make the same sound?
*
Yesterday at the door she brought you to me.
So many days of travel, being shown off,
you'd barely slept, eyes red
with fighting the touch of strangers.

On a whim, she lifted you onto my back,
we stepped outside and your cries stopped.
Tracking a bird you grew there, cooing,
your head falling so lightly in toward mine.
*
In hours, on your way home
across the mountains, the plane will rise.
I know. You'll arch like a swimmer
to your mother's breast and she'll pull you in.

From this still dark hour I approach you,
as if I were there, as if words had weight yet.
The sounds you make are small
thwips and cluspings, and gripped from inside you

the cry you need, for the dark space, waking,
for blur and loss and your truculent will.
Listen now, coiled one,
the morning's gone blue,

creeping in behind the pines.
My two-celled light glimmers
a small planet on the asphalt,
on the brick streets.
*

Tomorrow, below the curtains of your room,
you'll watch the light make streaks
along the ceiling... like a floating stage.
How the blue horse on the mobile rises,

mane trumpeted down far ranges and cities,
the walls spinning into motion
like a sea. These are the tasks
that will hold you here, rituals of grace,
rituals of fear, the watching,

so that in a way you can never go back
to the sleep you knew, the fond unknowing.
Even there, overhead, the geese would be honking,
and on the wide blue back of *all*
you would be riding.

Starved Rock

The forest's edges widen
  into oxbow
     where white trunks blur
  branch onto reflected branch
like wax melded along a string.
My brother and I ran
  this world once, where
    we'd left our father sleeping,
  the trail rutted like a spine
    along the rim
of the eroded cliffs. Buried under
  the joints of a canyon
  the face of the Horned Man
    cowered between two crevasses,
  his mossy brow
  triangular and twisted
below the weight of his many beginnings.
  Maybe this was our father
resurrected within the strata.
    Surely we knew little
of the legends of these bluffs,
the Illinois stranded, Pontiac dead,
  the French promises
     withered to their cold roots.
  Here their last passage,
  their one entrance and escape, rises
one hundred and forty feet
  above the river. They must have known
    the outcome of the choice,
  to cross over as if sealing
themselves into the sky.
How their enemies would gather
  all around and under the cliffs,
    merely wait, then move in.
  In the end many dove, they say,
  rather to face
the hunger of the rock
  than join the slaughtered ones above
     like bloody offerings.

> We scattered bees
> in the red-floored pines,
> stumbled a trash pit,
> a sand road down a gully.
> In the campground, found our father
> awake at last,
> and stirring the fire.

Children's Drawings
in gratitude to Robert Coles and
Their Eyes Meeting the World

We choose, almost always, the solitary figure,
hence our passion for the sun, which waits, we say,
here, behind a smudge of clouds,
or smiles at a squished angle

above the teacher with her glaring eyes.
Here is a "voof" (they ask:
a "wolf"? No a "voof") and its dish
of blue food. We come to listen for the names

the figures give. And always
where the light comes from.
Red glow around the head of an angry nap,
or slipped through the cracks of the purple flower—

these are the gaps we slide between,
wishing to swim. Where do the hands go, when a hand
draws a hand? At the side of the head—or extended
toward us as if grown from the belly?

A hunger we feed, this smear of color
set down to serve the route of a shape,
to make the world, head
sunk into legs, link up again.

Here a spy bides in black stations
past the green of his hidden home. Here the blue
swaths of walkers, bent in their columns,
ascend across the blue-dotted snow.

The Baboushka Poems

In Russian legend, while sweeping her floor one evening, Baboushka is interrupted by three figures who invite her to join them in searching for the Child. Although she at first refuses, later she goes out to find them.
   When she can't, their tracks drifted over in the snow, she travels the world leaving gifts at every doorstep.

I. Baboushka Raises the Child

Here they are alone—no magic carpet.
But the child wants to know
how the gifts revolve—

how each figure nests inside the last
and is forgotten.
Such questions, Baboushka laughs

and folds the child closer. She's learned
the sea-change of stillness
within love. *For this,*

there are no words, she says. *One enters
as the other leaves. You'll know. Sometimes
the tanks arrive to urge you on,*

*sometimes a tune played blindly
behind a window.* Baboushka raises the child
till their hearts are level. A swallow

slips through the lacings of the bridge. The sun
laps once more the world round. *We begin in circumstance
and end in song,* she knows—but doesn't say.

It's the same message everywhere. The water
sputtering. The hands locked. The imprisoned
sleeping in the darkness like the free.

II. Baboushka Sweeps Up (At the Homeless Shelter)

She wants too much, she has decided,
for love to be clear. Rather the grains of this floor,
the shreddings of last night's newspapers,

the cupped ping of a February morning. The hot
water pipes rattle like prisoners—
no equilibrium for them. And the friendships of a night

spill into the bitter favors of the city.
Each day she wants them back, each night the stench
and talk, the moanings in the dark send her out

in search of stars. She is a five-legged spider
whose web rips as it forms. No sex
can pull her close. None of these wayward

children are hers. None has ever grown with its head
at her loins, its mouth needy at the loose riddles
of her breasts. How could she find again
the sweet ache in her heart to travel on?

III. Baboushka Finds the Statues of the Wisemen Outside State Auto

When she first opened
to the knock she thought *only wind.*
The broom grew to her hand, and the dark

room turned. Three times.
Then they were clear,
in the spark it takes for a red roar

of pine kindling.
She said *no* but the next day
came out, their tracks drifted over.

She wove small gifts from an endless skirt.
Dolls with blue and brown mixed eyes.
Heads of husks pierced and glued in hovels

far from Kiev. She packed her bones
through the gathered cities, eyes dim
with the stitches of the highway.

And never thought to find them so,
above the gleaming hard black sand.
With the others she warms her hands tonight
on the glass of the spotlights.

IV. Baboushka Dances at the Summer Lights Festival

Well, it's been a long way. She's full of numbers
she can't explain. The long highway of *one*,
those dozen years at the heart's hovel. Now she's brought

a stew, and a tidy mound of bread
and a dress trimmed with what was once
the language of heaven.

The floor extends their feet, and she joins
each hand to another. The cotillion stringing all
of them through like a looped

free knot. She catches the click of her heels
in the mothers' eyes—a sudden wish for
the parlance of wonder. Here, again, at the top of the world—
no end—as she steps round.

THE RIVER'S DAUGHTER
-her word, in love with the shore-

Patterns I saw in the current—thick rivulets
like women's clothes washed out
centuries below where we sat
along the thin ledge of memory,
a little dream of us
when the dark was just beginning
to break.
*

I fear: the otter's sleek joy,
lightning slash, rimless flood
of all the seventh years.

The noose they brought once
and that mad boy who twined out along
the slick branch
like a snake—they—

I run from them, slip back down
into my naked scrim, swim
just here—at your heels.
*

Mother was the Empress.
I heard her evenings purr,

their brave little bridges—their thirsty traffic—
seal me in sleep.

I've watched her eyes blinking and the doors
of her meals part open the trees.
*

Burning house on the riverbank—
the bendable flames rise,
lap the blackening planks—
shadow of a mother

calling to the shadow of her kids.
I know I cannot control you
any more than this flame,
ruse of teeth the world hides.
*

Mornings I lay in our white bed
head filled with melodies of trains,

striped as a clam
worn ivory by the water.
*
In my dream we climbed up to crystal chairs
and found the wind condensed into twisted ripples
out along night's floor

and the charwoman who daily
hammers out the stars
handed me a chunk of congealed meteor.

With gold trays the others
(like her) passed, their black clothes thick,
light winding—

cherries in the night
hung just over our heads.
*
I am a window covered
with white cloth.

I wander out onto the ice
where it breathes below me,
its little bubbles
too small for mirrors.

Under my feet the knives glide
over the distantly remembered water.

Wrap around me
in these coats, love,
your winters.
*
Loose rungs paint-
dropped and the apple tree

already leaving its
shiny eyelids on the shore.

My body urges
its way up

into your enclosure,
our time sealed

to crisp orbs
in the mirrored budded branches.
*

Where does the world lead
when it's so lightly woven,

when it digs at time
as we do with crusty hands?

And when we trace these lines out
of loving, is there no end

of combinations and recombinations—
foils of loose and rippled skins?
*

My skin is only water.
*

What I want: the snow's retreat,
night's high collar in a storm,

the name I had when I could not yet speak.

The wings I heard
in fierce flutter around us—

stone at the ark of the valley
where you called me up
to sit beside you,

one lit room
one slice of window.
*

Gingko, my ribbed heart,
my thousand-heart

yellow assembly—soft bank
of earth—why should I not fit
your flutter-pulse?
*

But I do not belong here
where your mitered fingers

fold the edges toward becoming.

Listen to how the subway cars
rattle their tunnel homes—

I too could be gone like that
evaporated into a sound.
    *

Now what I carry—
the statues of ash.

I *am* her—I become her—
mother-river—the arch of me.

The mist-hours stretch their firm sides,
lay long in the path, where I slip aside.
Rows of long shields
gleam in their white sea.
    *

Then come close—a last time—my grass name.
In the quartz wind—even at the end—
you scrub away at shadows.

I know another music now
of shattered coils
measured in cells of grains.

Above us one whisked seed
like a red flaming eye
rides—trapped— into this harbor.

We make a world where it floats,
drifts along and shudders
like a tiny boat.

Tonight the rain
will drive it down.

The Theft of Silk

On the trails of the northern Himalayas,
beyond the cliffs of Jade Gates Pass
spring was said never to go.

Xilingshi stood in the Emperor's orchard.
There was a laugh inside
those mulberry leaves.

Three thousand years
they held her secret, the moment
when she dropped the cocoons in the water

and the webs spun out
their white wonder—
her own cloud.

Leaves of one species—
that long memory of veins, opened
even the caves of the Buddha.

And Persia—fountain, fortress, middle land
thick with knowledge not its own, selling
out of tents those wind blown bolts.

A woman in green enters a plain bedroom,
no painting, no walnut bedstead, but she has on silk
and it's as if she's been enfolded into another skin.

Only a few are allowed the stage of wings
for when they do they must break
that seamless white strand of solitude.

Justinian I (550 AD) spoke to the monks (his spies)
and they brought him, risking death, the eggs and mulberry seeds
hidden in the shafts of hollow bamboo canes

beyond Wei and the Yellow River
through Jade Gates Pass, where for centuries
spring was said never to go.

Notes from a Season along the Olentangy

Early morning: cottonwood down
drifts the river's limestone shelves into pocked
and half-filled hollows.

One fat carp between the reeds
stirs a cloud in the river's shadows.

Vertical from the reservoir cliffs
a hunched turtle rises, limbs spread
and softly rippling.

Men in fatigues dip and scatter
like sandpipers
fishing what's left
of the current below the dam.

Long afternoon I am nestled
in the splintered roots
of a dry riparian maple.

All day what is alive moves in the leaves
like thread briefly closing the spacings.

A voice (mine) calls into the observatory dome—
and another, disembodied, answers.
I come up like a diver into the airy space

and the ghostly astronomer narrows my eye
to the double-star glimmer
he's been plotting all month.

Clouds shift: just under the reservoir's surface—
a school of larva-devouring catfish, after a rain.

Frogs when I pass at noon
skitter halfway to mid-stream
and still have room to lift
their eyes above the sludge.

The moon half-scoured out, like a melon
tipped over, pours also
nearly empty.

Kathy says I'm crazy. Some nights along the river road
I turn off the headlights

and let the car ahead pull me
with its flickering halo
through the green-then-dark canopy.

THE GOOD HOUSE

Blue eye above the earth
rides east with us. No rush, we
have the whole day.

Steam lifts from a farm pond
like a wide white tree
stretching its roots in the water.

Deeper in the hills, buggies spot
the towns: Berlin, Charm, Mt. Hope,
each with its Narrow Lane.

At the egg auction, wide with bleachers,
cartons mounded with brown shells, ours
are the only uncovered heads.

Gravel crossroads. Willow roots
above the draped stream.
We ask directions at the metal shop.

The father strokes his wire beard.
Outside, the youngest daughter plows the air
on her horseheaded swing.

On a slope above the edge of town
the good neighbors lie.
Yoder, Bessom, Gretzenmueller.

Ragersville: The Good House
stands like a yellow ghost
right up against the road.

Hair tied back, ex-biker, the cook
sits down with us, his legs bowed
around the chair, the wide room empty.

Laughing, he brings us a single dish:
thick slabs of spiced portabello
with a side of edible flowers.

2.
SUMMER BY SUMMER

"Sunmotes lilted around them like yellow butterflies"
-Truman Capote

Half-Sonnet: Sunday

The island mends itself with broken shells.
Our invasion is nothing new, timed

to the centuries, the palm of the moon,
gray cedars reclaiming the quarry, white scars

of the ancient crustaceans scraped raw
by machines that are themselves now gone.

What is real? What cannot be said—the lake's cold
heart where we hesitate and, at last, curl in.

SEA TURTLE
(Columbus Zoo)

Frying pan of pressed clay, I cannot retrieve
my head and neck, for the thick muscles
flay out my limbs like oars.
I wait for hours, motionless, a forest,
a fierce plug at the bottom of the pool.
Wait with me, entangled currents,
measure of manatee heart, veil of the ray.
I am the motor of the sea-green yearning,
head without voice, cadence of below.
When my upper body thrust
drives me surface-ward, four legs
puppet-wide, contorted, exact,
wherever I am always returns,
as now, the sea its own wake,
the passages predicated on whim
and turn, balance and refrain.
Whatever I forget comes back to me
as method, ache, reach, release,
my century a womb beyond light, my entrance
a weighted circle, my agency a spell for rest.
Slower than light, you would not mistake me
for a shining coin or a celebration,
maybe a continent, a lost range, a soldier
gone calm, barn owl of bleached memory
below the hooked face of the sea.

Train and Ocean
for Colleen

A deep ache follows travel, as if trains
rearrange our bones, replace them with longings
of iron, minor tunes of crossings played
over in our sleep. Late night gatherings,
delayed arrivals make of time an unfamiliar
home, memory-less, as the days unfold like light
across the bay—three bridges strung to the peninsula,
mouth of the Susquehanna, Havre de Grace to Turkey Point.
What guide will stitch back who we were, give name
to change and reappraisal? Pieces of sea glass,
tossed up like faint offerings, measure the grate of wave
against sand. Like them, when we've become something else
we'll know our weight, transformed past vessel,
broken, smoothed of edges, light as selfless selves.

SINGING TO NOAH
-deaf at age two-

He slips in the pool and twists under
for the first time, head draped
in a rush of water: now his body

knows its opposite, the lustrous need for entrance
and comedy, its seal-weight
roiling and oiled, spooled to the wake

of the rubber ocean. His mom has leapt into the midst
of children, hem darkened now, till he plops round and sits
upright. And she will laugh, and sing to him

this night, as ever, knowing he cannot hear her words,
any more than the body can know the water
it is swimming toward, and in: this

immanence he sleeps against, a voice
rocking and clear inside the bones.

Watching Isa Pitch

Her name fans out around the diamond
  and into the shaggy outfield grass,
so common now—as brushing beads of sweat
  away, she hears and does not hear it,

bears down on the next three and two count.
  The motion comes steady, placing her spiked
right foot nearly vertical into the groove she's worn
  below the mound, the left tilted back as if

she were on a roof and knows that on her stance
  balances more than her own fall. Parents too
drone in, "Pitch it pretty, Isa," "Wing it,"
  "Lean on them, lean." The words particular,

meaningless as swallows that skirt the distant
  cropped hayfield. Only her coach is quiet,
watchful, the lessons already taught,
  to be reinforced later. Hand cupped

against the seams, legs low but without that dip,
  back like a pole under the arch of sky,
but mostly this—an arch inside, steady weight
  and re-beginning, whatever this, whatever the next pitch.

Train to Glacier
*"Inside this clay jug
are canyons and pine mountains..."*
Kabir (tr. R.Bly)

Beginning in Cleveland, we project ourselves into a light,
    some blinding headlamp as unrecognizable at first
as an echo, a pealed circle of sound

    minored into warning, into an iron track
tacked to its rocky, rocking bed and banked
    into the tunnels, the re-threaded

forests of Pennsylvania—one doubled strand
    unbroken from the sea—and here, in our
halved oasis, lifts us as if to braid us

    into our bedded, dimly lit
anonymity. We waddle, sleep our way
    to morning in Chicago, the crowds at State

and Michigan mirrored in their glass. How many
    muses passing, and how far away?
Eat our lunch under the thorns and fountains

    outside the raised and corridored museum.
And now the prairies wait, with their long-encoded suns,
    the strands of the upper Mississippi

plaited at dusk, crossing and recrossing. Red Cloud,
    Fargo. Each town progressively smaller,
strung by mere luck to its wailing mother

    line. And we collect stories, signs
on giant posts that hover over elevators, speak
    out into the night. "82% of North Dakota

soybeans are fed to cattle." This
    a boast, to be stuffed inside the steaks
at Ma Rainey's Ranch. We collapse

    into our passive ride, choose no exits,
neighbors. The puffy teens headed home to Seattle
    with their tiny screen feeding them

  endless movies. Their hovering father desperately
    honing in on their lives, offering them apples,
old plums, while they down a parody of breath,

    and how many myths? We cover more than half a nation,
  map the hours with successive games—
    and not once does one child ask: how far,

  though the days lock and rattle,
    bleed like county lines. Ponds grow sparse,
  sloughs balance on the contours of depressions

    as if the bright doors in the land
open at will. Arroyos. Sinks. Wire
    strung gray as the shorn grass.

It's August. But we're headed to the ice.
  We want to know what's living
at the heights of this desperate continent,

    what breaks from crust to hold the rain,
frozen basins brazen against the cracking sun.

This Day's Thirst
- for the Cuyahoga Valley -

I retreat to this room because it's where I can go.
   What remains of someone else's coffee
grown cold on the counter. It's the first or second

day of summer, depending upon where you place
   the turning of the light. Down the path,
a frog's found his way below a slate of algae

which from one angle really is as gray
   as a highway. Here the trucks take short cuts,
hundreds of feet above, the overpass hovers on stilts

at the Empire's command. Below, there is a quiet
   singing I'd forgotten, as if like Pan I'd split from my shadow,
coming back to find it here, locked upon a tree.

Words slide in and my hand must grasp them
   somewhere, turned inside out, as if inside were feathers
and all I had to do was breathe to let them fly.

Solstice at Kendall Ledges

Walking inside the walls of this thin cave
halfway before the vast theater of the rim,

I listened at first for any leftover voices
and found only this spring

talking inside the rock.

Darkness had begun
to find its fingers;

the others on their way to the moonrise
had wandered on.

If I could reach my hands far enough
across the gritty crevice, I thought,

turn my head in tandem

to catch a shadow flitting out,
maybe some part of me

would already not be here.

That would be good—
there's plenty of me already

to worry about my feet
getting wet, how I might get wedged in

by the briefest of tremors.

Overhead, the designs of the fallen
had let thousands of years

of soil form within their loss,
the persistent roots of cedars

wedge toward whatever angles
they might find—

and so would I,
given enough courage,

no matter if I fell too far behind.

The sun would learn to come down anyway
and break across the ledges,

the full and floating moon
sliding over the trees

would split open a wide meadow
for those wanderers

to sing their way across
without a single measured path.

Skipping Stones with Noah

Streamers from the sun lay down upon the river
and the trees settle in for their late August roosting.

Noah checks my hand to see how I'm holding the stone
then slumps when his next throw trails off to a thunk.

With so few words he carries his memory of the world
in the twists of a trunk, a full body twirl,

his hands above his head to trace the hollow of an eddy,
his arms chasing the heron's thin flight.

Tiny clamshells gather their detritus
in dry pockets along the river's slate shelves

and opened, set on the bobbing scrim,
become such temporary boats.

Tonight the river is ours,
though two fishermen have left their chairs

as if to save their places for a parade.
And that is what we are, what this shallow current is,

as we choose the thinnest stones, approximate our balance here
all the way to dark, trying to conjure that single glide

where the hand or the toss or the riding slate itself
has nearly become the water.

Bagworms in Their Tent Above the River

Reversed architecture, translucent
spun body: from where I sit, like a worshipper,
the sun lights up your tunneled womb
encircling, honoring even, the leaves and limbs
which you destroy. Thickets of tiny worms
collect in the pockets of your tilted circus home—hardly more
than hairs crawling, burst down the narrow, swung arches
like ringless, leaderless thieves.
I have burned your kind before, in my early age,
stripped web from orchard notch with a gasoline glove,
sometimes a single apple, like a distant tumor
inside a breast, hanging within your ghostly
elegance—or plunged the whole lopped branch into the burner,
a kind of hellish pleasure in the shrivel of those
death-hands as they climbed the black walls
of the flames and fell back in. Is yours
the same feast, though slower, more attentive and content,
branch by branch the tree stripped down
within your sealed city? One loose coil of a child
falls from a strand, lost it is
and nodding at the wind, one tipped finger
on the farthest ivory key that finds it has moved
beyond the realm of sound, where another weaver
slides through the silk to drag it safely in—
as the thick of the fire hauls back
each orange and bickering tongue.
Beside you the scourged branches of a previous
victory hang, black and pealed, blistered raw,
still rippled with your sting.
And already in this enclosure the bones of leaves
hold their scoured forms, dull lamps
or limbs off a fetus born without a spine. Like them,
I could not slay you, though I lived within,
eyeless bodiless emperor who even now
releases spy-spores toward your next reunion,
summer by summer will never let us out
of this gorgeous, breathless, woven room,
without edge, without beginning.

3.
Eight Riddles

*"It's not so very late—it's only dark.
There's more in it than you're inclined to say."*
-Robert Frost

Note: Each of these riddles describes an ordinary, everyday action, using metaphor-based clues. First clues, scrambled answers, and the answers upside-down can be found on page 48.

1. For the Day

Reaching in blind
you leave sight for those
who know better,

lifting the limp soul from
its iron lament. Long it has
hung, like a vessel

in safe harbor, unsullied,
unable to grasp
even the simplest of stories.

So you stretch your sleepy arm
into its enclosure: sheer
air within a flight tunnel.

Now two, to make for wings
and your shoulders itch
their way in, testing the color

this day will carry, as you count
the hard riddles of ivory and opening
rising one by one.

2. Limbic Construction

Lounge at the endless edge
of opposition: the loose

and the formed, the lucid
and the dense, where once your body

sought its first name of motion
and now scrapes together

a firm hour's decay. You've walked
on this whale's pale eyeless side—

a flesh that gives
like flesh itself

and records each step
for the depth's reversal.

Several hands now join yours,
to raise the smooth floor

against its will, formed
of its oneness,

imprisoning its multitudes,
shorn and pressed,

leveled and raised,
held together by what will soon

drag it away.

3. The Deceivers

You and the one you must kneel for
balance on the bridge
that is no bridge, which only trumpets

a single, plated note to let the blue symphony
begin. But the blue isn't so blue
really, not now as you look through

layers of glass to where the quivering
digits of greed answer
the slightest call. Yours

is their hawker, parading whatever wares
you could find, underground
or far within the keep,

your shadow-heir now
wands—to sway hypnosis real,
slip through vagrant migration

and pluck the one who will soon
wave homeless, stolen
from the vanished mirror,

speechless but desperate for words.

4. Incantation for Departure

Something is still that is made of fire
like a month that has only begun
in the mind. Trimmed it is

with September's gritty radiance:
what you once knew returned, to be lifted
like the thinnest bandage with the plow

of your shaving hand. No mystery.
Here is a shell beneath, the world's hurtling
retreat, loose womb or tomb, self-

tracking with quivering measure.
Now you are within the sealed mind—
only the bit of angled flint between your fingers

must enter the thinnest cave
and snap the trap's gap. Listen
close. There's a giant asleep before you

gritting his teeth, waking at his only name
repeated as many times as you dare
till the waves begin to roll—tiny buried candles

burst over and over: monks of viscosity
and monks of the desert meeting in streams
from their long dark corridors

to light your humming prayer.

5. Two-Headed Cadence

As if you were made in a world of change,
its pace your own, stable only

below, in the bound and sliceless sabers
where stoppage is not allowed,

where motion dictates
aquatic breathing, teaching

a home to the you-that-is-not-you.
It is as if your head had a journey

you will begin a thousand times
when you forget the second step—

and so must return
to that absence

which is momentum, that self-
deceptive choice which never crests.

You are no more
than a psalm at the lost

beginnings of speech, speaking all
to the one bound at your midst

who has already left you—
who knows your voice as its safe,

single tunnel into dark,
your measured heart as its one

name for time.

6. Courting the Address

And so begin to bend,
    reaching to tie
your left shoe
      and stop,
like a tower that stops
    just before
falling, then sway back,
        toe pointed

and arched, as if
    inching out
to trip someone,
        and while your left
hand slowly offers
    a drink to the sun,
swing your
        right arm

back and up
    on its loose pole
connected to a pin
        on your shoulder
till above your head
    again it stops,
as if pointing
        a dagger

down your spine, jerking
    forward—
like a sledge
      hammer
hitting the water
    or as if you were
handing a paper
        to the king.

7. The Accordion

Here and there are not so irreparable
that the eyes cannot reverse themselves to find—

———

caught within ascension –
a funnel of the will.

———

Reflex and forgetting
parade the vertical corridor within

———

this binary mooring, inviting the cantilevered brace
to call its brother on.

———

Rising and flattening, monochrome painting of stripes,
brings a thin land, then another

———

in geometric plains
the breath begins counting.

———

Emptiness unfolded, trust—the mortal name—
repeated until nothing is the same.

8. Lessons in Trust

At first we are speechless, wedded
to stasis, though we jab at where we
do not want to be.

Then we are free
and the pages of the world open
as if we were—always—their center

no matter our direction.
It all depends upon these wands—
their steady blending

of surface and depth,
the rhombuses and trapezoids
our arms make

with their awkward incantations.
It's as if—from above—we're combing the hair
of the wind, smoothing the tangles,

now worrying out a knot,
probing ease and deliberation,
the push of the *given*

against the smallest
angles of the will—
so sweetly we are held

above reflection
and the luscious dark
carrying us on.

Clues And Answers

Right: First clues
Below: Scrambled answers
Bottom Right: Answers in order

First Clues
1. For the Day
    Within the dark: apparel
2. Limbic Construction
    On the shore: such temporary rooms
3. The Deceivers
    From the planks: the stolen life
4. Incantation for Departure
    In the drive: will and resistance
5. Two-Headed Cadence
    Rhythmic journey to sleep
6. Courting the Address
    At the edge of rectangles
7. The Accordion
    Habitual column: below & above
8. Lessons in Trust
    Gliding weight

Answers Out of Order
Walking up the stairs
Building a sandcastle
Rocking a child to sleep
Canoeing
Teaching a child to fish
Starting a car in cold weather
Putting on a shirt
Tennis Serve

Answers in Order
1. For the Day = Putting on a shirt
2. Limbic Construction = Building a sand castle
3. The Deceivers = Teaching a child to fish
4. Incantation for Departure = Starting a car in cold weather
5. Two-Headed Cadence = Rocking a child to sleep
6. Courting the Address = Tennis serve
7. The Accordion = Walking up the stairs
8. Lessons in Trust = Canoeing

4.
CROSS-STATE

*"I will take with me
The emptiness of my hands"
-W.S. Merwin*

Driving Northeast on Route 42, I Cross Under a Double Rainbow

From your home town, the one
you keep returning to each summer
as if you have to yearly walk the ground there,
the one where I had gone to school, its smoke-
stained limestone cliffs above the sluggish creek
and sad, dissolving center
my first true taste of America, I drove
away from you, all the while wanting
to return, to gather up the days
that we could make, burrow inside them
as if there were no time, as if they were all time,
trembling, as when we climbed the spikes
of the cemetery fence, your skirt just leaping free
from tearing, the gravestones
inseparable from the gray of the cliffs
and the fallen leaves of our desires, spilling edgeless,
the evening sun nearly doubled,
squeezing through the trees
as if it too were being poured into some huge
exploded mold, its form recumbent,
its mystery unowned—all this
I drove away from, before me
a roiled storming dark, turbulent rising
threatening blue, behind, an orange
December sun, far to the southwest,
throned and molten as your hair,
and pulled to the shoulder
in the slanting rain,
stumbled up the roadside rise,
the arc of doubled rainbow lifted, real,
where our split worlds met,
licked the rain from my dripping face,
lost and opened, found and banished,
the road ahead unnamed and moored,
the one behind sustained, equivalent.

In The Fields of Oil
-Roberto Lopez (Lyons, Texas, 9/28/80),
photographed by Richard Avedon
"A portrait photographer depends upon another person to complete his picture. The subject imagined, which is in a sense me, must be discovered in someone else willing to take part in a fiction he cannot possibly know about... these disciplines, these strategies, this silent theater."

Avedon says
      sometimes talk precedes the flash
and he can't tell how long the story will have to wait

for its one moment against the white sheet.

Five summers he roamed the Western light,
as if it were a wilderness still

in the drifter's eyes, the carney's. Unemployed
black jack dealer,
              workers grimy in the oil fields,
stained in the strip coal mines.

All entering his terrible borrowed light

as if they'd been severed
from the very land around, or stunned
while peering through his lens.

He props himself beside the tripod,
not stooped to its black hood
              (where old magicians
made the burst of faces appear)

and so becomes

a silent figure
standing in his portrait's place.

      All this Thursday's coal
dug in Nevada
and shipped by train

will light the city of Atlanta for eight
hours of Monday.

You can't see these numbers
here

but you can stand in their absence.

It's what this bright
and fierce eroding
                    light was meant to do.

Roberto Lopez, oil field worker,
latched
into his black straps at the end of the day,

like any wayward Orpheus cannot turn to see
the drama he's stepped out of—

the scrim of the oilfields
                    burning off the signals
of the sacred gas, which for so long
have escaped us.

Around his neck
like a strange and birthmarked collar—and down

        a central column
        of his chest, dividing

lung from lung—a darker stained skin
haunts the tenor here.
                    How far
is it from fire to fire? From your face
to your body to your life? In every county of America

the wild rides lift us
till we whirl away,
as Calvino dreamt, the carnival becoming the town
and the workers move in caravans down the lonely roads.

Who owns the road? The scaled land? Why are we
so willing to stand in front of the stranger's vacant frame?
How many floating continents must combine

to form an earth, an ear? How many scars
of knife or horn or ferment must rise

to fence one level of us
from any other? In the fields of oil

maybe we can only
be lonely. Maybe every song
haunts, every round, scarred imprint, like this one

just above his highest rib,

may become a mouth,
a vagrant cell
where death can enter. In the fields of oil

there are some shadows
                        which can only become
                        our eyes.

My Mother Above the Abandoned Quarry

Jagged limestone boulders
shoved to make
a necklace for the quarry

form dozens of precarious stairways down.

The wide and supple hands of the bulldozers
sent off long ago to rust
could not scrape it clean, left these

impromptu cairns, crevasses for cedars,
this throne for my mother, in her final summer,

to watch her many charges
scatter
over the moonscape expanse.

Even my father is her child again,

awkward hat on his head and wobbly
as some toddler, his legs gone
so white
they're almost blue.

We enter: windless bonsai garden, red seeds
spread by waxwings, dense-star flowers

rooted through the rock,

aqua-alkaline lake at the base
of some cragged island fortress without foe,
reeds at its edge.

In two hundred years

how lush it all will be,
this unearthly atoll. Braided cable wires
like ripped out nerves.

Split shells blanched
to cull again the sea. All the treasures

we carry back to her, as if she could bless
the ragged world all over again,

trembling with each name.

One More Rainy Morning
In memoriam, Bob Fox (1943-2005)
-writer and musician-

The hours are disappearing
   as you drive back to Dog Holler,
      your beat-up, sway-bridge southern Ohio farm.

You know a story waits there still
   if you can arrive in time to type it out,
      though it'll be raining in the morning, you can tell.

There's your great-grandfather,
   who swam, they said, for the Czar.
      Twenty years later, he wasn't swimming,

holding his breath among the dead—
   another pogrom—spreading his children
      through moonless nights, across guardless bridges

toward the West. He is a half-face now
   as he turns to cross the highway. It's getting late.
      People will be gathering inside your home to sing,

your neighbors and the ghosts
   of Jelly Roll Morton, Leadbelly,
      and the Rev. Gary Davis, whom you led

through N.Y. subways when you were nineteen
   and he was too blind to make it to his churches
      and Greenwich gigs alone. They'll be listening for your tires

on the drive. And the red-faced preacher
   hawking *God's Roast Beef Sandwich—if you're not too busy*
      to take a bite. And the restless man in the supermarket line,

slowly removing from his spine each white
   and exquisite bone. They're all you. You bring them all along,
      knowing the illusions time must break, allowing

even your parents to brush off the ashes and scars
   from their Catskills hotel fire, calling you
      to bury them, to take your own place on the scales.

How is it, then, you are so weightless,
    no torque to the motor, no grind on the curve
        that bypasses the basined city's lights, the sky so dim,

the lights on the barges so slow
    on the bend around Pomeroy? You won't make it,
        you know that now, a thousand nights and songs

will have passed without you. Your children
    will have your urn and spill a little more of you up and down
        these hills like seed, saving the last wash for the Atlantic tides.

Silence will be soaking through the layered roofs
    over all your cities, your beloved farms. The singers
        will be going home, so tired, in the early morning rain.

CONSTRUCTION
for Ed

Long drives down the numbered nameless roads of Ohio
   through the corn with its furious green flags
      protecting the bellies of sprouting nubs—to work

these long days covering the decaying houses of the farmland
   with pleated plastic swaths locked and angled like a puzzle
      to keep out the rain. Or else laying block

into the severed ground, humping their gray and gritty carcasses
   down the plank, delicately angling the plumb, and sometimes
      ripping it all down when the lean got too bad—

it all gets into us like the two-note call of the jay
   we barely hear, until the morning grows still
      and it's only our hammers echoing out over

the yellowing beans. All day a wind keeps up, your scheme
   to turn your father's farm into a tidy cash-crop
      of apartments begins to sway like an unsecured rafter

under a defused moon. It would have been so easy,
   the remaining mortgage paid by these monthly turrets,
      the woods and caves salvaged, your mother's last years—

but the walls are always sinking under your ideas, the crew
   is slow—or late—and there are these three girlfriends
      who bring you to their beds on the way back

from the lumberyard, the hardware, and the sound of hammers to me
   will always be a hollow one, more filled
      with the emptiness below than any driven coated

weight, the darkened digits riveting a wall,
   and when I remember you, there is always
      this huge roofless, sideless scaffolding

warping and beautiful where your dreams stood—
   and I climb up inside, as if into the belly of a ship, my hands
      unclaimed, my right hip weightless, and so much want to float off

into that unchristened sky, and over your dead
   father's fields toward the harvest moon, not even
      needing to wave goodbye.

The Yellow Spring
for the Glen—and Tara

We wandered, slightly drunk, off the trail
to the place that had always taken us back,
where in July the fireflies
throbbed thirty-foot columns through a stand of oaks,
where we'd lain
some afternoons in the fair
haven of the pine forest,
reading with our heads propped
on the same log.
Or drank in tandem from the Yellow Spring,
that bright fountain made as much
of bronze earth as of water.
Were we lovers? Yes—but of this place, mostly.
I knew you only here. Even our arguments
found trails. When I told you
of the old man I'd come upon
who'd hung himself with his belt while
standing on his bike
in the woods beside my suburb,
you snapped *that was his right,*
that the children who found him first
needed to know how far sadness could go.
We stayed away for months
but finally had to meet
under that slim limestone outcrop
where you'd first told me of your daughter's death,
how your hair turned white in a day
when you were twenty and she was two—your Jenny—
crushed beneath a neighbor's car
where she'd been playing the game you'd made together,
arranging stones along the bumper,
when suddenly it moved
and she was underneath, her eyes on yours
before they closed for good. How you lived
in that same town for years—blaming yourself,
walking through the open blame of others,
or had another child—is more than I could say.
We went on, courting the rocks, the way
water rose within them
and poured out in hidden streams. Each time the Glen
was new, stepping through its open doors
it was as if we were greeting ourselves again
or some selves we had lost

too many years back—so that now, a nearly warm
December night, we made it only twenty feet
to the edge of some drop-off
we could barely sense,
lay down in the thick leaves,
and not knowing it was a night for meteors
began to count the falling stars.
Dozens came—the Leonids—but we thought in that hour
they were just for us, the only ones watching
the heavens rain.

CROSS-STATE
for my father

Long ride down the middle of Michigan, the car a single bullet
dropping through space, the two of us inside.

He says nothing for miles—or, more often, the same thing.

We fall through a mirror with another life inside
where he enters endless hours of his own beginning.

Like Willy Loman, this was his territory. He designed dozens
of bridges for crossing these shallow, brackish streams.

So we avoid the blinding throughway, take the small
back river roads—once his, now no one's.

The mirror shatters along the angles of its story
where the beams brace, where the sky breaks, where the dark fish rise.

Where the green must be hidden—if it hopes to live again.

Strangers and generals long promised him a world,
a grief frozen the exact size of his clothes.

He will not return from these clouds,
from the lake of sky, where we are driving.

Where these sticks form a web for crossing,
held by sweet suspension at their core

as with any bridge—as he knows, stepping from stem to stem—
that center being strongest which holds nothing at all.

After August

A year ago this day I heard my sister's call
as I packed the books into the car to head
to the museum. All day teaching in the galleries
her face—our mother's face—turned from every painting,
Henri's golden-shawled dancer before the dark curtain,
Noland's hazy target of penti-colored sound.
Two states away she'd had another stroke,
August already weighted so deep into its round.

At dusk I started driving, hardly aware
of the hurtling exits, the cars that summon their burning
from where the world began. I plucked a tape
at random from the case behind me,
listened to Greg Brown's *Poet's Game*
the last thirty miles before her room.
And there met my brother—my own brother—
who hugged me for once, bid me sit with her.

To have a daughter, what is that? To follow
in the footsteps of a son? Once we begin, what choice
do we have but to pour the water, set the tea
into its darkening? Still room, turned dark,
the hospital lit with its tiny budding emergencies
for sleep. At midnight the nurses urged me home
and I slipped into the late shift traffic from the factories.
I'd come to the end, I knew, of *The Poet's Game*,

began to fast forward to the other side (a crazy
wish for such a time) but stopped it—reach out
my hand and stopped it, perhaps thinking
there was some other song I'd missed—
and my mother's voice came on
talking to my daughter about some dream she had
for the world, what I'd always most teased her about,
her thinking we could all get along. My mother's voice

like some pentimento of sound behind the tape
I must have recorded over, like a painter covering
the past, leaving this lost fragment, her voice in the dark
as I drove along to sleep in the home to which
she'd never return, talking to her granddaughter
from her vanishing room, her voice squeezing back to me,
in my blindness, the only way it could.

THE PARIS ROOM

My hand must have touched
the glass, a foggy trail weighting its path,
down that pure membrane separating
the city from the room—

      outside, the walls of Paris,
  so pock-marked, so crammed,
  curved like a cathedral,
      buttressed by the graying
  years—

your face within, that could pull
fur from flame.

Mid-morning, the kids back in Ohio—
nine hours of ocean in between sealed like honey

  in this honeymoon for
  the already-childrened

and this hand (mine?)
reached out
and wrote
in the residue of us—
a shower, two,

  I love you
  in steam that I thought
  would disappear.

  And we went out,
your face was flushed, or was it mine—
    as I recall
  —how many mornings had we
    been there,

getting used to the tiny elevator,
  the fierce stairs,
  the grim blue-suited consierge.

You wore your white dress once,
  I know that, your veil,
and I bought you a rose
    from the vender who came in off
    the street

    into the restaurant with its sheer
glass walls,
        crowds milling in the Paris night.

  Some of them applauded—
    I remember that—
  I don't remember
      if I bowed—
I know you took
      the rose
        in your teeth.

And it was that day—
  or another, earlier, or later—
    the days like strings,
    crystaled with
      the knots of us—

for we knew we would
         return,
  that these days were but a
  ruse—
    to tie us, make of us
    a cart to haul
  the years—

and it was that day, or the next
  we came back in

to that golden room—it seemed golden—
    in the evening, or any
        Paris afternoon.

  Someone had answered—the someone, I suppose,
      who had changed the towels,
        and made the bed
        and cleared the mirror,
    someone
    below, in the steam still clinging
        to the
        glass

    had answered, in
  another hand.

5.
Eight Inkblots

"A creature that hides and 'withdraws into its shell,' is preparing a 'way out.'"
-Gaston Bachelard,
The Poetics of Space

INKBLOT #1: IN THIS TAVERN

The theory of inkblot
   rests in its absences,
     its symmetry, the icy-white channels

  that slide between
the black: islands
    immune from language

that like a film rise up across
    whatever vacant screen
  they choose. These two

  ghoulish heads, perhaps,
frayed as continents,
   philosophers,

above the empty space from which
    their bodies
  have been disposed, appear

  almost smiling, or is it toothless,
still enough
   that birds are already nesting

in the folding bridge
   between their hair. Then who
  are these jokers, sharp heads

  and flapping beaks,
oblivious to what hangs so starkly
   in the callous

night? The tavern
   is closing,
  its mirrors folding until all words

  drip slowly into their
stumble-mugs
   and the ghostly bar-keep raises his arms,

some kind of prayer or cheer,
   balancing the dead back
  to their cave of ice.

Inkblot #2: Mr. Double-Eyes

All skulls, all shovels, all shields
double. All swimmers. All minds.

Even this shabby cap of Mr. Double-Eyes'
that drapes his head like muskrat hides

and allows him to pretend to think—
or see—his upper set of pupil-less flickers,

his cortex slumped
to a flimsy tongue

dividing his pointy lobes. It's like
he perches—as we all—

upon his nobler self—or selves—
the push-me pull-yous

that rock within our sea of worry
and wonder at our troubled nights,

and do their twinned and starry best to shine.

Inkblot #3: Combatants

    The inkblot's core
is separation—or else

the thrust of union: countries
    with their speckled zones

    that betoken wars
or forestation—splitting along

the invisible faults
    of a shrinking earth.

    Two kings—or misers—
bickering, or praying

or meeting at the center
    long enough

    for the leap
and slap of palms, then

shoving off—their robes awry
    their locked glares forming

    the bead of a spider
spun from their sameness—

what each sees
    and despises

    in the other and is
unable to leave.

Inkblot #4: The Rivering

The theory of inkblot necessitates
    the fold, symmetrical or radiant

as a shaft of sunlight
    splinters through the water

and this lost segment of the river
    is a turbulent, turning jewel.

For so these creatures catch
    themselves ensnared—a masque

you can distinguish anywhere
    if you look long enough

into the hours : nymphs or sprites
or peg-legged centaurs, costumed leapers

holding up a wand, pointy chins
or toes lifted in one leapt-step,

droopy hats: divide and blend,
    exchanging fluids. And if

there's only one
    propensed for looking back

who's left his face afloat
    for his partner to snatch midstream

we'll never know for sure
if it's his fear of falling upward

or his love for where he's rising from.

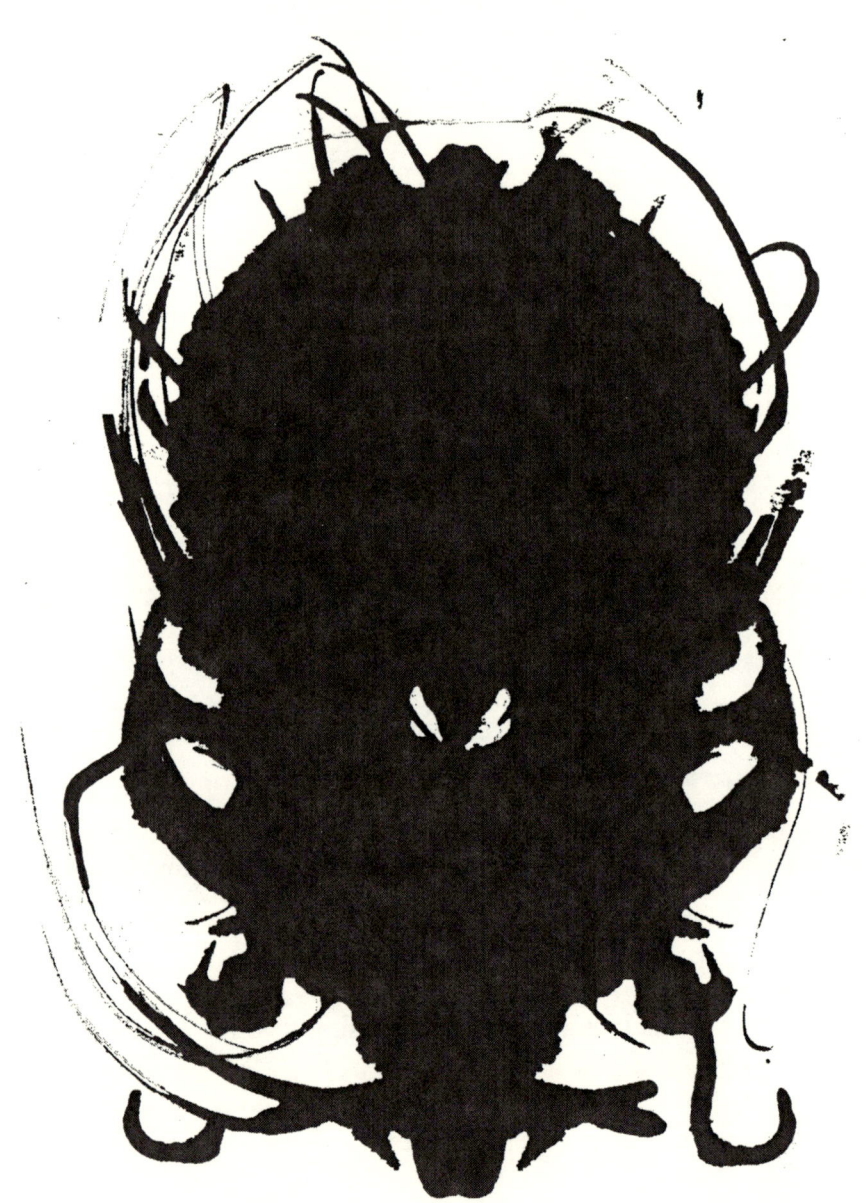

Inkblot #5: Scarab

A face behind the mask?
She's nearly beaked,

one eye lobed and crenulated
the other hooked

to catch the sleepers.
*

More wolf
than wise, more wild
    than boned,
*

the inkblot throws its flare
    into our faces—

its husk at times too thick.
*

Today let her gather and reshape
    the mind—sacred scarab

bound to eat
what heart has left behind.

Inkblot #6: The Forest Floor

The theory of inkblot coagulates
  desire, on its wide white plain,
    unable to be

more than it
  receives of the dark—and must look always
    to its brother, however distant,

for what it
  most believes:
    Who else will arise here?

  Two sentries of the bleached, divided mist
two musicians
    inheriting a theme,

burdened
  in a language,
    as tendrils sprung from seeds:

Around the stalk
  is imitation
spun,
    creased

into mutation, that slide-
  step dream
    which may, with luck,

lead
    just as well or better
to breaking through

  the burial
    of the leaves.

Inkblot #7: Trumpeters

The theory of inkblot dresses the shadows,
   shaping twins to ride

the devil's swing. In calico frocks
   and clumping boots, they trumpet

whatever dawn or sunset might arrive
   across the ivory floating field. This call

that dark chance conjures
   from the pool inside its spurious well,

dripped and folded, centered, sprung upon the page
   with a single clap, a muted

slide of palms, a toss of molten coin
   to redefine the day. And at the core?

ambivalence: some tyrant
   with his yoke to keep these angels

moored, or else, in mortal longing
   perched to save his life, listening

(quite beyond himself) for these rising chords
   he'll hold onto while falling.

INKBLOT #8: DANCE OF THE SINGLE-WINGED

The theory of inkblot
   predicates
the uncreasing

  of the wings, their caped
dalliance,
    their tendrils strung with flesh.

From ancient days
   the drapery sprung:
but how to fly

   when there is only one?
The years
   have burdened even

our walking. Our merest
  touch threatens,
our wines are

ragged in the throat.
   Yet look, love, when we meet
we form a mirror

   anyway, configuring how,
with these weaponed
  appendages, we will learn

to feed each other—
  and risen on no other
point of balance

  here in the air,
swing ourselves
   to flight.

6.
DISAPPEARANCES

"And then, forgetting what she wanted there,
Too full of blossom and green light to care,
She hurried to the ground and slipped below."
    -James Wright

The Mayor's Promise

Into his rooms too the rats crept,
nightly gnawing the arches over his fire
or his bed. So when the knock of the pied coat stranger
broke the deliberations, he knew where the coins slept

but not how the children would follow. The mornings
are quiet now. He has time to trace shadows
across the ceiling or turn as the light grows
fierce inside the mirror as on a spit of its faint string.

He has time to swallow days, or curl
inside a promise, bend a moment till
it prays, lay the shoes out for the lame

boy, who was too late when the stone door closed.
His, the after-wisdom, fingers on the dark holes
of the silver forgotten pipe, that plays two ways.

THE SATYR AND THE PEASANTS
Jan Lys (1600-1629)
The National Gallery

The satyr's arm ripples like a root. The hair at his chest
forms a cross or valley. He wears a wreath on his head,
and a wreath at his belly. He tilts his tipsy head
to look at the baby and the baby looks back,

squirming in its mother's arms.
His laughter like the plunk of his hooves
is too loud for this small tavern room.
The patrons look on, and consider if there's

cause to interfere. The only light is from a small window
behind, and the fire before, the central figures
(nearer to us than the rest),
a fire we cannot see—

it lights the satyr's skin till his neck and hands
are the color of sandstone, from his neck to his hands
the same color as in the baby's face, the mother's
smooth flesh on the rise above her breasts,

the father's disbelieving, upturned face
trying to eat his soup.

Child Aloft in Ohio Theater

You do not know the headlines or the daily fate
of others with weight and size and eyes like yours,
lifted from their cribs till their lashed necks shake
and their senses are battered dense by their fathers,

who would sleep. You do not know the plot
of the movie, or the myths embedded in the bronze heights
above you: Neptune and the Sirens, shined bellies and breasts
beckoning to the sea's court, to lights

more elusive than these above our heads
ablaze from sudden red horizon (at intermission)
that draw your body from its makeshift balcony bed
to ride aloft there too as your father suns

you, in a little leap, as he lets you go,
legs an inch from safety and his fingers.
You rise again, with the slightest toss, then in air slow,
fall to his lap like lead. "Again," you say for the lure

of separation, magic pull of those rayed stars,
rippling gold streaks up the backlit wall
as the last spot dims and you dare
to laugh, having hands in which to fall.

Terre Haute

Walking toward the needle of his execution,
his non-remorse emitting the gathering tribes.
Spring has long overflowed the walls of the Midwest,
the eaten green tower, the steel grid age.

His lack of remorse, a mirror for the tribes,
for the moon to return to its wax pool, to dream,
to swallow the green tower, grid of steel-spanned streams.
We have to become what he is, they say, and sing.

Moon trickles down to its pool of wax.
Clouds burl and knock at our wires.
We had to become what he is, they said, and sang.
The placards hail their jests, they call for flame.

Clouds blister, knock at our wires.
Spring has overflowed these wide Midwestern walls.
The placards hail their posts, bitter their flame.
The needle, the eye, the walk, the cloistered execution.

Another Fourth

Why not suppose here an end to the war
in spidery munitions lighting raidless days,
impressing on the sky these scarless scars?

The crowd trades home for wide, exploded stars
that melt into a silvered disarray.
Why not arrange here an end to the war?

A deaf child edges the roadside tar,
spins with each flash like a dark atom strayed,
summer pressing on his brain its windless star,

alive as him, with green extended arms,
as the bombs escape, explode and fade.
Why not toast with them an end to the war?

From here, all sound explodes far
off, like bright-launched shadows entering the bay.
Summer passes like the brain's deep scar

approaching its close, its packed repertoire
of losses burst in shimmered rays.
Why not dream here an end to the war,
on the midsummer sky a hundred scarless scars?

Four Psalms

1. Dance

At the bandshell by the river the crowd
packs in: molded couples blend blanket
to blanket, which she slips through, swallowed
into the sound. She grasps her awkward, lanky

lover by the neck, arms looped,
swaying to the spotlights. The root-squelched,
August-thirsty ground echoes the skewed riffs,
lash of drum—like a drum itself

in its sunken arc, or the very curve of time
she worships, with something more than prayer
or pride, the ache of all that passes, glides,
pours up and through the throbbing air.

2. Witness
(for Valentin Gatynya, 1932-1997)

So there he hung, where we—or anyone—
might find him, above the altar (keeling)
of his basket and his bike, his tongue
already thick and black, the tree

bent low, a good strong willow,
as if to give a grim permission
or point us along the mud-slick hill to
be his witnesses, his first, guessing

that what some children, from their untended hour
along the creek, glimpsed through the trees
was him, was real. And stood our best before
his breathless choice. Silent now, Valentin.

3. Invitation

I have been reading. Now the bells ring *seven*.
Last night my daughter went out to see the stars.
The day begins at so many points. What's given
depends on entrance, propulsion of years,

blend of wedding or mourning. She takes
his hand descending the front steps. Couples
older up and down the street rebuff and shake
their doors, as if to ward off bears. And love is

emptied by the pail it filled. May we forgive
the apples in their rounding, reddening foray
into what might be. That *was* might stumble into *this,
this, this,* and light ferment its shadows into day.

4. Song

Good mornings gather around the garbage
set out each Tuesday, as the cabbage moths
and suburban, long probed monarchs range
the zinnias this still-chilled fifth of August,

or words exchange languages—the French *guard*
becoming (for us) *keep*—jagged with error
and passionate relief. In the park, stained, scoured
rocks parade the river, like a mirrored

city where the wind tips its rising
scales, one shape of cloud or fist or tongue
invented from another. A parcelled green
divides the reeds till they widely merge and strum.

GHAZAL

All night I sleep inside the crumbling walls of cities
and hold my cup up in the morning for a taste of words.

Summer dries the tongue while in the garden
wavery ears of the eggplant shape a new land of words.

My deaf son, with his portable ear turned off,
watches me and cannot tell my anger from my words.

Prairie flowers steep beside the driveway, goldfinches
born from their shining disarray—like words.

The teacher takes his cloak off, all the distinctions of the year
spilling from his sleeves, the mannequins of words.

Everyone was speaking, age their excuse, coins
their disguise—a hand of dust erases all their words.

I turned, my name entering its last fever,
its shape as wrinkled as a path. A hill. A face. A word.

Credo

The walls are lonelier than we believed,
whole towns are swallowed through them.

Whole days bloom inside rays of light.

The road has a memory and creases its perfections.

At the first step of its first traveler
the shattering of the earth began.

We wind the earth within our worries,
release the horrors when we ignore (or trust) our dreams.

I believe in shale, its daily shattering,
in what grows moist, letting the water through.

In cold that claims the hours,
in shelters made of bones.

In numbers that form vacancies.

In riddles that consume our homes.

Geographies press at our dissatisfactions,
winters curl inside rocks till even breath is ancient.

Pools form in the skin.
What we begin one day may bless the talc of exile.

Sex is another country
we enter mostly through transgression.

The pen is a substitute,
the page a conspirator.

No matter what, we carry puppets;
no matter how, we bury fires.

Each one who leaves leaves open a door.
Each word braids another wave.

To be alive is to enter an ocean.

The only exit is a reversal of our names.

The only languages worth knowing
are scratched in ash.

Magnetic ripples fold into our eyes.

Our eyes are a pure emptiness that space alone redeems.
Our hearts, when truly ours, are richly hollow.

To Eakins
"The Gross Clinic" (1875)

Now at the other edge of history
  it would not be so odd to place
this doubly-sliced and twisted
  poor man's thigh before us, gray socks
    nearly the same color as his skin,

draw down the ivory light from
  the good doctor's cranium to reflect
in the sterile cloth below
  and the gauze-cloud above the patient's
    hidden head. A minor tragedy really,

demonstration at the poverty hospital
  for the troops of medical students,
white-cuffed and glum, hardly visible
  in their tiered amphitheater
    but for one, leaning casual in the corridor

and the pen of another, red
  as the doctor's stained fingers
as he pauses, gaze bound elsewhere, as if probing
  the right words. But there are no words,
    it's just the withered mother does not want

to see, her hands before her face tangled
  at what you show us (and she knows):
that the pain comes twice, and no amount of ceremony,
  aides in suits like bankers who kneel to apply
    the ether curtain, can hide from us what's to come.

DRIVING HOME
*"Daddy, when we get to the top of that hill,
are we going to disappear?" -in the car, age 2*

Midway between Mt.Gilead and Shelby,
Route 314 dips low to the Clearfork Reservoir.
Several lights like paired fates
flip up or over the ridge across the valley.
Weary from months of teaching, I slide the car
out of gear and coast down in the dark.
In the backseat, now ten, my daughter sprawls,
for once glad of the hour. And her mother,

turned chin, shoulders, hips and knees
to her window, is silent. I am silent.
Held above the earth, in its late season,
in our small orbit, bent to geology,
what consequence? We rise over the gap,
my only, and yes, we disappear.

7.
MIMESIS

*"And Polo said: 'The inferno of the living
Is not something that will be; if there is one,
it is what is already here, the inferno where
we live everyday, that we form by being
together. There are two ways to escape
suffering it. The first is easy for many: accept
the inferno and become such a part of it that
you can no longer see it. The second is risky
and demands constant vigilance and
apprehension: seek and learn to recognize
who and what, in the midst of inferno, is
not inferno, then make them endure, give
them space.'"*
       -Italo Calvino, from Invisible Cities

*"The daylight is coming, Henry McBride—
I am going up on the roof and watch it come."*
       -Georgia O'Keeffe

Mimesis: The Nighthawk

Years ago. Some mother bound it,
  brought it to your classroom in a shoe box
    where it hunkered, strained

the cardboard edges, cross-stitch feathers
  like the fit of shadow-patternings
    along the forest floor. At home,

you lifted its gray head so that its mouth
  flexed as if to form words for the deaf.
    We knew it nested the flat roofs of the city,

swallowed gnats, invaded swarms open-
    mouthed. We'd watched dozens crank the sky
      up slowly, stories at a time,

then drop wings in sharp descent
  and here—such cowering, mouth
    clamped to fight the dropper. That night

I took a broken sleep: child-launched rocket,
  trail of wings, funnel through the aerial highway
    and your dim image where the wind would be.

What were the boxed hearts of those roofs
  that they once rayed all our caring—lights blurred
    down a brick valley, sides sucked in

like enclosing bellows? It's been twenty years.
  Yet walking last night, I heard them, their shriek
    above, where the scraped-thin blue

of August darkened, knew them
  almost without looking up,
    as the blind must shiver

the hum of traffic at a curb,
  or trace the measure of their fingers
    over the hard, raised braille.

Prairie Burn
for Lynda

We stare
into the grasses, the path
   we've come to know
by seasons: the prairie,
       narrowed from its empire

to this eight-acre plot
behind the campus. Yellow-orange,
   gold-brown, red-rayed stalks

slip by us, and each other,
till it's nearly some tufted hide
whipped round by wind,

tawny shouldered, pulled back
or driven forward
   in single movement—or a thousand—

as light turns quietly over
   within light.
    *

The growth points hide
   —from swept fury—and sprout each spring
into green stubble

against the blackened land.

Three months—and these thick grasses
over our heads
   as we push through

their incessant joining.
Bluestem and switchgrass bend
   to tunnel dance,

swaying moon, stayless surface
   of bones and seas, loam and till,
landlocked, unplowed,

thronged
with their own hum.
   *

Spring—the tinder matted—
we gather
    upwind. Hoods of firefighters

pass within
the grasses and around the edge,
rocket vole

and rabbit out with premonitions of flame.
    The prairie waits, a dazed creature,

till the south lip takes
hold. We wait: a bit of
gasp, then thick

orange canyons rise from the air.

No, orange*ness*
rises, its fierce breath
   *

on fire, flames that call
and answer in one blade,
    ground lightning, lap

of the devil's tongue,

ash magician, fierce coat of the sun—
    let the smoke rise,
this god return

to wherever it burrows
in the earnest
linkage of cells, long sown, long

winter-dried, and here
    so fiercely,
ravenously burst.

Path to the River

Dusk: the dog owners mill near the paint-peeled
    pavilion, circa 1965, free their sleek
or shaggy charges to sprint in pairs

    or tussle mock rage. Elemental gathering—
mock tribe on a warm October evening
I pass before I blur into the river willows.

    The eye is the wick of a candle
moving before the mirror of the still
    and inside the yellow-green flame of fall

wait two descents. In my dream of the stage
the crew had built a river—
    and I kept saying: *this is a real river—*

sweeping right to left, the table, the limbs,
the wagons pouring in. Here, the trails bald
    with use: always someone to arrive,

retrieve the dog, sway to the wayward
    branch. Love churns this way,
six months collapsed into a year—

    as if we could ever hold back the banks.
Now what is not here beats as loudly
as what is, as if the book of us

shook loose half its words. *Chthonian.*
    Reverence. My head against your belly
as the showerhead rayed down.

    Bones along the tracks
still cling to make a jaw.
    A song rides by, habituated

    to its airtight chamber.
    The juggler beside the path
on the way to the university (no path

that does not bleed into another) reaches for
    seven when five becomes
routine. He senses

us watching, as the numbers cohere, unite
until the click, drop, rise of them
    arcs a light as easy as our days.

The eye is the mother of bridges, tests
    each strand of the horizon,
the apples that fall—ripe or not—something right

    about the sound they make
        against the hollow ground.

WHEATFIELD, JULY

One stem alone is more intricate than cities,
its roots thumbed deeper, threaded with grace: so

this day unfolds its fevers. South Wind
training the flag to a quivering July.

To choose the day is, always, to argue with the sky,
lapsed as we are into its circulation,

substituting one brief wish for a constellation
of mornings. The stones in the far cemetery,

propped above these Ohio fields, cluster, are our own
rooting, the clutch of our spaded hands on the earth.

*

The wheat does not move much now,
locked as it is into its fisted rustle,

each kernel, with its nearly transparent veil,
so small yet toughened to its turreted wall,

pebbled to the gold sea: months of colors
gemmed to this one ferocity of plains-knowledge

to be danced out, shivered, melded
into segmented glowing hours—at our feet.

*

What deliberation? I am *within* the idea of rain,
the thunder not yet announced,

the furthest branches of the mulberry
from out of the woods lonely as asters.

What I thought was the wheat's alone
was really the day's: the roads tuning

their slim vials, the harvest held off
as a wedding, nothing to be hurried,

like an ace shifted within the sequencing
of hands. The wheat steadies its musing hands,

regards its marriage, the possible storm
of the day, its coming brideshead harvest:

What little wombs to spring from soil!
What thick gatherings for knowing, for rain,

for the clustered thistle flowers—
so brittle now. And ready to be done.
*

So I will lie here until the words come,
till they are pyred with grief, with the piercing

of roots. Death is growth: each day is nearer—
the implantation of regret twinned with shelter:

Choose this home, this breeze, these weeds at field's edge.
I am the sleep of days, the drum of hammers

for distance, the eye for the infusion of want,
leveled to the knee-high wheat. Give it all then, the falling away

of intricate beckonings. The dry kernels
hum and spread their tents, like soldiers before the war.

One Love

In the hall they meet—though neither is much aware—
   and talk about mandalas around the xerox.

At first lunch, she has to leave quickly
   but later that summer they ride the doubled Ferriswheel

swung over the contraptions of a temporary city.
   First snowfall they stand on the edges of the third floor

window and talk of Florida and the need
   for a deeper change. By February they speak of marriage—

other people's—the confines of the expected bed,
   decide that now they can talk about anything.

But it is listening he wants to do—he says—to hear her
   down to the gray of her eyes. Above the muted

Ohio gorge, she touches his beard, and everything—
   even hair—seems rich and strange again.

They buy a book on Jung together, while a drunken
   or nearly drunken man leans in to give his opinion

and they hug and she is on a plane and now
   there is the feeling of never having let go.

Lost on a highway at night—the intended
   destination ghosted—they eat at Ann & Tony's—

rain and the near-miss of oncoming cars
   all the way home. "Let's talk"—"Let's be careful"—

they brush lips anyway. High above the tiny stage
   their hands slide soft to intertwine.

One kiss in the car—and under the oldest tree
   in town and in the museum of masks

each tells the story of who'd they be.
   On the floor of her apartment

she says without his shirt he's skinny as Jesus
   and later they are bowling with the mock-cries of the pins.

Backwards over her head at midnight on the asphalt court
    she sinks a twenty-foot shot flung up blind

and at the bar they trade childhoods though the years
    wait at the door with their coats of rain.

Night walk in the cemetery—her father in a dream—
    jazz over wine in Cincinnati—a blanket under pines.

Spring is still cold—five candles sway a room—
    there are kisses that lightly pluck his chest

in his empty house under the blinds' shadows.
    Who is here—a train pulls through—woken at night

by storm they find each other but not the same—
    and soon the walls are gone. A month of distant

separate places—unbuttonings swallowed down a phone—
    night after night imagined pools that loom too large,

screens of letters that gather their hands.
    The closer he pulls the more she slips away—

darkened conversations along a highway—his family there
    and she comes—a stranger illuminated in a sudden light.

Summer dries the grass—she has entered—the door left open—
    lain down upon his sleeping back—and stars drift across an island,

confessions in a quiet bed—just before this long divided
    slumber—and the wondering where did they go.

BECAUSE OF YOUR WHITE SHOULDER
after Bei Dao

Light strums slow over the curtains
a photo of the blur of trees.

I'm done with collecting heart bandages,
smoke from that summer's fires.

We ride on the edge of buried numbers,
the paleontologist's hopscotch.

In the long afternoon nap, the moon slips
off its round and climbs in with us.

Your body shakes in its dream beside me,
divided into its tiniest memories.

Every musician unlocks the road
whose address is the address of the snow.

The old storyteller kneads the dry flesh of his hands,
the oil thin at the bottom of its glass bowl.

Every story speaks of this one—a tiny wound
which spirals from the splinter.

So now (as if there were a now)
I touch your shoulder as July opens.

Cold, a birthday of hatched storms,
kisses above the river.

At Isa Lake: An Epithalamium
for my daughter—from the place of her first naming

I sit on the shore of your tiny lake
   and watch the vagrant light move through the branches,
   no more able to be held back than

the wide rivers that begin so quietly here.
   Half the water lying so brackish under the lilies
   will be spooled to the Atlantic

down the wide and slow Missouri,
   half wrinkle west toward the coast of the Snake
   and the Puget Sound.

In this beginning space, where can we place
   the blame for anything? The scrim of your name swells,
     the droplets with their inventories

nudge over the tippled ridge
   of the invisibly plotted divide
     each year when winter heals,

when the rubbery red stems receive their tilted
   exact angles of sun. That say: rise.
     That say: riggle. Fill this haggard range,

spun earth-chiseled channels
   with threaded filaments of narrowed breath.
     There is no seam, yet everything is stitched.

Nothing disappears, yet everything collapses.
   One path leading down through the fallen pines
     might transform to journey, might call you still.

Cross over then—and let the maze of currents hold you
   where they bend into the always green-veiled morning.
     Linger in this continent so long and wildly skewed

and find the words for *love*, that is, for *onward*.

PEGASUS
for Christopher Merrill

The underside of the apple's leaves turns silver.
Night filters its calm over the farms.
The moon is late. An hour after dark
I climb the ladder to the black ship
of the garage roof, and lie long inside
the crush of galaxy: there's the boy

who broke his father's chariot loose from the sun,
and Cygnus, this swan, who pulled him
from the river. Sagittarius, Andromeda,
Pegasus, his great box-flank and head
above this summer's closing shop.
Long days I've watched in swirling winds

blond strands of sheaves rip upward, twirl slow
mute distances, like dreams suspended twenty feet in air.
And what reason is there for a poem to you,
except you've come back twice in dreams...
once carrying a code of inlaid speech,
your poem rayed outward like a blue cell dividing,

and later standing at the base of the stairs
past which all talk became a mountain trail.
Days of rain will soon have whittled
the sycamore bare, and for the first time I'll taste
no sweetness in their curse, tracing the dead
tangle of branches in the obverse dawn,

for the first time knowing: it may not come back,
this staff of world carved to minute reliefs,
the borer's routings under bark, all could vanish
like the code of Mayan books under singed
Spanish hands... if we stop watching.
Come then... dress the seeds' fall,

slap dust of shoe on dust of trail,
out past the chatter of crowds,
contracts and the plumes of planes,
cities sprawling with speech and bludgeoned
speechlessness... where the bold horse rises
above the auto dealer's glare. It wasn't our name up there

we wanted anyway, or a chance to ride
above the sun, but a ledge from which to watch
the grandeur, the shudder of those wings.

Love Poem, August

Three a.m., the stars mold a rounded knowing,
beating on the inside. Restless,

we leave the kids to their sprawled
telegraphy, the windless whispering,

and lay a blanket between the cut-shadow
yards. There are meteors:

we've come to watch them stripe the sky in brief

pale music. Now that we've known anger,
do we touch different hands,

seeking sleep and finding only
its interruptions? When I held Noah, at ten months,

in front of the huge orange Rothko
at the Phillips, he stretched his hands up

as if to greet you—or the sun—
as he did when I'd lift him to the hotel mirror

and he'd dance, going nowhere. So we
greet ourselves, love, in the far streaks

of these stones, crossing
from space through the tight flame

of earth, in order to be seen.

Acknowledgements

Journals

Antigonish: "One Love"
Earth's Daughters: "Driving Home"
Fourth River Review: "Sea Turtle," "Rituals of Grace, Rituals of Fear"
Hiram Poetry Review: "Watching Isa Pitch," "To Eakins"
The Journal: "Children's Drawings," "Pegasus"
Orion: "Mimesis: The Nighthawk"
River Oak: "The Baboushka Poems"
Rockford Review: "Starved Rock"
South Dakota Review: "Bagworms in Their Tent Above the River," "Wheatfield, July"

Anthologies

Orpheus & Company: "Pegasus"
O Taste and See: Food Poems: "The Good House"

Previous Chapbook

Child Aloft in Ohio Theatre in *Men & Women/Women & Men* (Bottom Dog Press): "Driving Home," "Child Aloft in Ohio Theatre," "For Samuel, At Seven Months" (as "Rituals of Grace, Rituals of Fear"), "Pegasus"

Illustrations

Section 5 Inkblots: Author

About the Author

Terry Hermsen has lived in Ohio since 1972. He has a B.A. in English from Wittenberg University, an MFA in poetry from Goddard College, and a Ph.D. in art education from the Ohio State University. He currently teaches poetry, composition and literature at Otterbein College. From 1979 to 2004, he taught poetry all around the state via the Ohio Arts Council's Artists in Education program, with students from kindergarten through high school, as well as senior citizens and other adults.

For five summers the author was on the faculty of the Antioch Writers Workshop—and he taught in the first five years of the Ohio Arts Council's Experience of Writing summer workshops for teachers, co-editing (with Bob Fox) the anthology which grew out of those years, *Teaching Writing from a Writer's Point of View*. Additionally, he was on the faculty of the OAC's Summer Media Institute from 1998-2003. He has taught poetry in the galleries of various museums throughout the state, including the Allen Art Museum in Oberlin, the Toledo Museum of Art, the Cleveland Museum of Art—and for seven years was a guest poet with the Columbus Museum of Art's DepARTures program, guiding 5th graders from around the city on poetry writing tours of the museum.

The author has published numerous articles on the teaching of poetry with *Teachers & Writers Collaborative* and *Teaching Artist Journal*. His poems have appeared in many magazines, including *Descant, South Dakota Review, The Journal, Antigonish, Confluence,* and *Orion*, as well as two chapbooks with Bottom Dog Press, *36 Spokes: The Bicycle Poems* and *Child Aloft in Ohio Theatre*. With David Garrison, he co-edited *O Taste and See: Food Poems*, which reached audiences all over the country through readings in restaurants in Seattle, Brooklyn, Chicago, Dayton and other cities. He lives in Delaware with his wife Leslie and their adopted children, Noel and Noah. His daughter Isa is a student at Capital University Law School.

Other Books By Bottom Dog Press

Cleveland Poetry Scenes: A Panorama and Anthology
eds. Nina Gibans, Mary Weems, Larry Smith
978-1933964-17-1 304 pgs. $20

d.a.levy & the mimeograph revolution
eds. Ingrid Swanberg & Larry Smith
1-933964-07-3 276 pgs. & dvd $25

Our Way of Life: Poems
by Ray McNiece
978-1-933964-14-0 128 pgs. $14.00

The Search for the Reason Why: New and Selected Poems
by Tom Kryss
0-933087-96-9 192 pgs. $14.00

Hunger Artist: Childhood in the Suburbs
by Joanne Jacobson
978-1-933964-11-9 132 pgs. $16

Bar Stories, edited by Nan Byrne
14 stories set in the bars of America
978-1-933964-09-6 176 pgs. $14.00

America Zen: A Gathering of Poets
eds. Ray McNiece and Larry Smith
0-933087-91-8 224 pgs. $15.00

Evensong: Contemporary American Poets on Spirituality
eds. Gerry LaFemina & Chad Prevost
ISBN 1-933964-01-4 276 pgs. $18

Family Matters: Poems of Our Families
eds. Ann Smith and Larry Smith
0-933087-95-0 230 pgs. $16.00

http://members.aol.com/Lsmithdog/bottomdog

Printed in the United States
129376LV00003B/27/P